THE AGE OF
DINOSAURS

Katie Woolley

WAYLAND
www.waylandbooks.co.uk

First published in Great Britain in 2018
by Wayland

Editor: Elise Short
Design: Peter Clayman
Illustrations: Martin Bustamante

ISBN: 978 1 5263 0420 9

10 9 8 7 6 5 4 3 2 1

Wayland, an imprint of
Hachette Children's Group
Part of Hodder and Stoughton
Carmelite House
50 Victoria Embankment
London EC4Y 0DZ

An Hachette UK Company
www.hachette.co.uk
www.hachettechildrens.co.uk

Printed and bound in China

Picture acknowledgements:
All images courtesy of Shutterstock except cover
image, p5 br; p6-7, p8, p10 bl, p18-19, p22-23, p24-25
illustrated by Martin Bustamante; p28 br Amazon-
Images / Alamy Stock Photo.

CONTENTS

IN THE BEGINNING

Planet Earth has been around for a very long time – about **4.6 billion years**. Scientists divide this time up into chunks called eras. Dinosaurs lived during the **Mesozoic era**, which is split into three periods: Triassic, Jurassic and Cretaceous.

Plateosaurus
[plat-ee-oh-sore-us]

Coelophysis
[seel-OH-fie-sis]

Triassic

Jurassic

| 248 million years ago | 205 million years ago | Mesozoic era | 142 million years ago |

Stegosaurus
[STEG-oh-SORE-us]

One of the **first dinosaurs** was **Nyasasaurus parringtoni** [Ny-as-a-SOR-us pah-ring-toe-nee]. It was the **size of a Labrador dog** and was discovered in Tanzania, Africa.

Dinosaurs shared their world with some **strange creatures**. **Eozostrodon** [ee-oh-ZOSS-troh-don] was a small, **egg-laying mammal** with short legs and a long snout – a bit like a **shrew**!

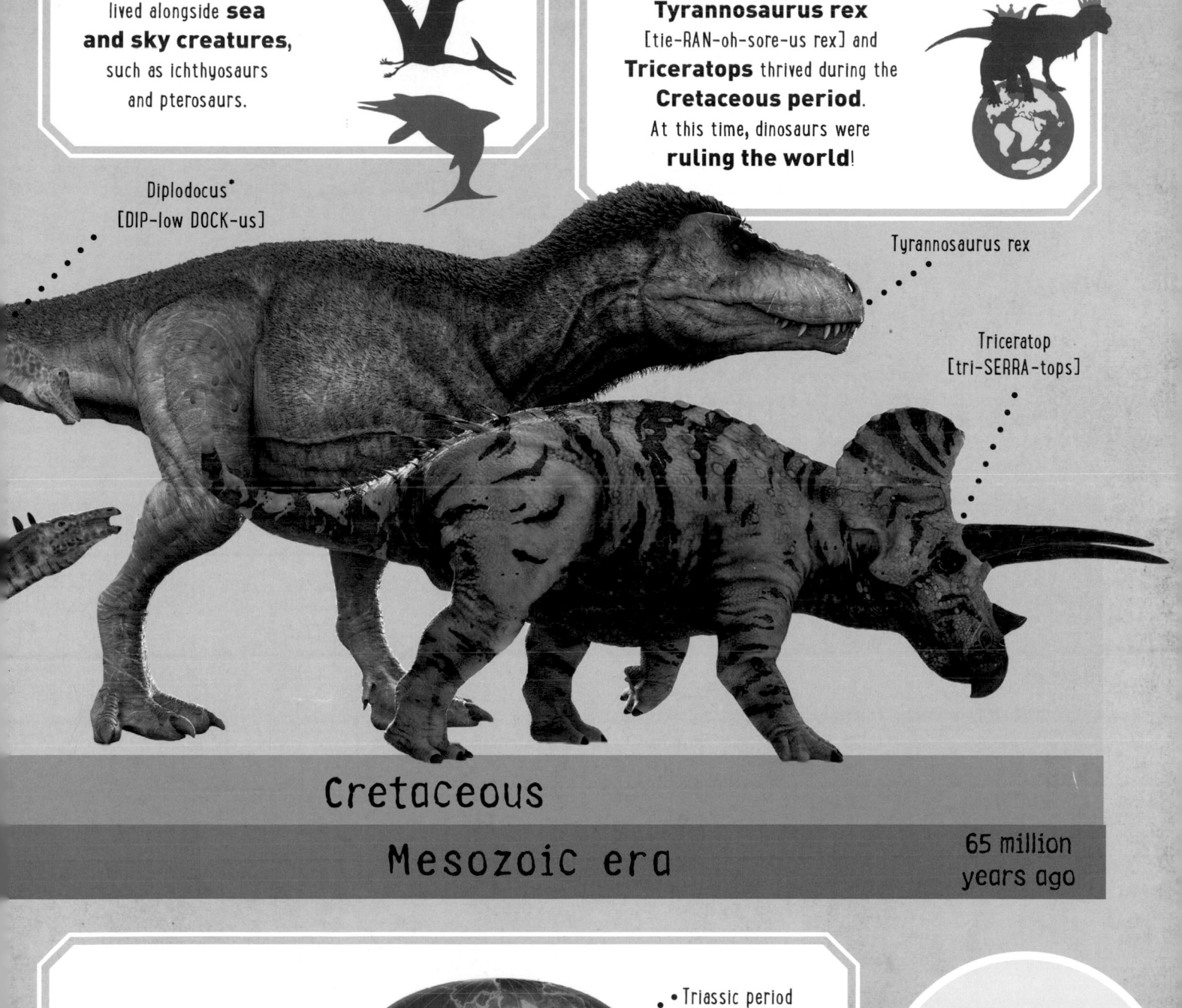

Dinosaurs also lived alongside **sea and sky creatures**, such as ichthyosaurs and pterosaurs.

Dinosaurs such as **Tyrannosaurus rex** [tie-RAN-oh-sore-us rex] and **Triceratops** thrived during the **Cretaceous period**. At this time, dinosaurs were **ruling the world**!

Diplodocus*
[DIP-low DOCK-us]

Tyrannosaurus rex

Triceratop
[tri-SERRA-tops]

Cretaceous
Mesozoic era

65 million years ago

Earth is constantly changing. Today, the world is made up of seven continents but the earliest **Triassic dinosaurs** lived on one **supercontinent** called **Pangaea** [pan-JEE-uh].

- Triassic period 200 million years ago

- Jurassic period 145 million years ago

- Cretaceous period 66 million years ago

Human beings didn't exist until **62.5 million years** after the last dinosaurs walked the Earth!

5

*not to scale

WHAT A VIEW!

Dinosaurs had a very **different view of Earth** from the one we see today. They wouldn't have seen any human beings, buildings or roads and they wouldn't have heard or seen any aeroplanes in the sky.

Pangaea was surrounded by ocean. **Pangaea means all the Earth.**

Triassic dinosaurs would have looked out on the **hot, dry desert** of Pangaea. This may explain why they **lived close to coasts and rivers**, to be near **water**.

Many **Triassic dinosaurs' habitats** were probably made up of **large forests** with trees and plants, such as **cycads** and **horsetails**.

The first dinosaurs saw **very little colour** - probably just **greens** and **browns** as there were **no flowers** during the **Triassic period**.

Triassic trees were protected by very **tough needles**. Their spikey leaves put off hungry herbivores.

During the **Jurassic period, Pangaea** began to **split** into two. By the end of the Cretaceous period, Earth looked more like it does today. Its temperature had cooled.

By the **Cretaceous period,** Earth had burst into **colour**! Flowering plants arrived and more **mountains** appeared.

Some dinosaurs may have eaten **grass**. Fossilised grass has been found in **dinosaur poo,** known as coprolite.

Late Cretaceous dinosaurs, such as Iguanodon [ig-WHA-noh-don], would have seen **magnolias** and **buttercups**!

WHAT EXACTLY IS A DINOSAUR?

Dinosaurs were **reptiles** that walked the Earth for 165 million years. Scientists think there were as many as **1,500 different kinds!** About 700 have been discovered so far. The scientist Richard Owen was the first to use the word 'dinosaur' in 1842. It means terrible lizard.

At the beginning of the **Triassic period**, dinosaurs were just another **group of reptiles** in a world full of reptiles. By the end of the period, dinosaurs **dominated** the landscape for the next 140 million years.

About 65 per cent of all dinosaurs were herbivores. The rest were carnivores!

Dinosaurs were descended from archosaurs. The fiercest archosaur was Postosuchus [POST-oh-SOOK-us], a cousin of modern crocodiles!

Some dinosaurs walked on **two legs**. Others walked on **four**. They all walked with their legs **straight under their bodies** and not splayed out to the side like a crocodile's.

Fossil finds (see p26-27) tell us about specific dinosaurs. Dinosaurs are usually **named** after the **person** who found them, a particular **feature** or after the **place** in which they were discovered. **Medusaceratops Lokii** [med-u-sah-SERRA-tops lock-ee] had horns that looked like the snake hair of the Greek mythical monster Medusa.

We are learning more and more about dinosaurs all the time. When a **fossil** of **Iguanodon** was first discovered, scientists thought its spike was on its nose. We now know it was on its thumbs!

This dinosaur is a plant-eating **Aegyptosaurus**, pronounced ee-JIP-toe-SORE-us. Its name means Egyptian lizard.

Dinosaurs had **scaly skin**. Scientists think some may have had feathers.

This dinosaur is meat-eater **Spinosaurus**, pronounced SPINE-oh-SORE-us. Its name means thorn lizard.

Aegyptosaurus was a **sauropod** - a kind of **plant-eating dinosaur**. Like many other plant-eaters, it had a small head, long tail and long neck.

Most meat-eating dinosaurs belonged to a group called **theropods**. This name means **beast footed**.

Meat-eaters had **sharp hooked claws** for finding food and protecting themselves.

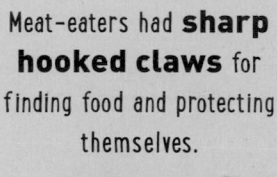

9

TRIASSIC DINOSAURS

There were no dinosaurs at the start of the **Triassic period** but plenty of dinosaurs had arrived by the end of it. These dinosaurs lived in **hot, dry habitats**, such as the Petrified Forest in Arizona, USA. This area is full of the fossils of Triassic dinosaurs.

This is **Coelophysis**, pronounced seel-OH-fie-sis. Its name means hollow form.

Coelophysis was a Late Triassic dinosaur. It lived about **220 million years ago**. It was **3 m long** – about the same size as a female **tiger**.

In 1947, the **fossil bones** of a **Coelophysis** were discovered at Ghost Ranch in New Mexico. Since then, the fossil remains of hundreds of Coelophysis have been found in the **fossil quarry** there.

During the Triassic period, dinosaurs such as **Coelophysis** were **not at the top of the food chain**. Large reptiles called **archosaurs and phytosaurs ruled the land**.

Like many small **theropods**, Coelophysis had **large eyes** to see its prey far in the distance.

Coelophysis walked on two feet allowing it to **run quickly and catch its prey**, such as **small insects** and **reptiles**.

Eoraptor [EE-oh-RAP-tor] lived about 228 million years ago. It was **smaller than Coelophysis.**

Eoraptor was only about a metre long. That's about the **size of a guitar**. But its sharp teeth and claws made it **a top predator**.

The fossil remains of a baby **Mussaurus** [moos-SORE-us] are some of the **smallest dinosaur skeletons** to have been found. This Triassic dinosaur **hatchling** could fit in the palm of an adult human's hand.

Among the first dinosaurs was **Saltopus** [sal-to-pus] – a very small meat-eating dinosaur found in Scotland. It was **no bigger than a cat!**

Early dinosaurs were not as big as later ones. But many dinosaurs had begun to evolve into bigger beasts by the end of the Triassic period. **Plateosaurus** reached about **7 m in length!** That's just a bit shorter than the length of a bus.

JURASSIC GIANTS

As Pangaea began to break up during the Jurassic period, Earth's temperature cooled, **rainforests** grew and shallow **seas** formed. This period saw the arrival of large, four-legged plant-eaters – the **sauropods!** Many new dinosaurs emerged including Brachiosaurus, Allosaurus and Apatosaurus.

This is **Brachiosaurus**, pronounced BRAK-ee-oh-sore-us. Its name means arm lizard.

Brachiosaurus held its head very high to eat leaves on the tallest trees.

Brachiosaurus ate about **200 kg of leaves and twigs** every day. That's like eating **200 cabbages!**

x200

Brachiosaurus weighed about **30-50,000 kg** – the same as **12 elephants.**

The **Jurassic period** saw the emergence of a wide variety of plants, such as **conifers and ginkgoes**. Mammals scurried along the forest floor as more and more dinosaurs stomped above.

As the number of **plant-eating dinosaurs grew**, so did the number of **large meat-eaters**. These mighty killers **dominated** the landscape, eating anything they could catch!

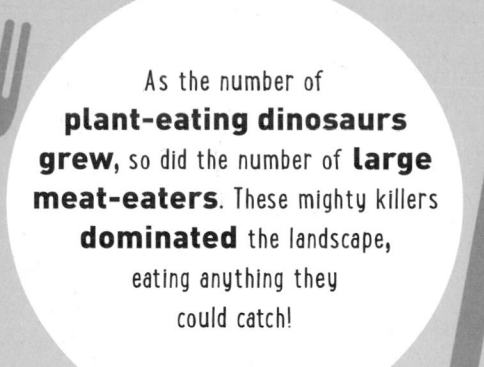

This large plant-eater is **Apatosaurus**, pronounced ah-PAT-oh-sore-us. Its name means deceptive lizard.

This fierce meat-eating dinosaur is **Allosaurus**, pronounced AL-oh-saw-russ. Its name means other lizard.

Its **long whip-like tail** acted as a **counter-balance** to its neck. It may also have been a good **defensive weapon**!

Apatosaurus was a Late Jurassic sauropod. It reached its full size at about 10 years of age and was **21 m long**. That's like seeing **10 male lions** standing in a line!

Allosaurus was a **fierce predator** during the Jurassic period. Its enormous size meant that it didn't shy away from **tackling big prey**, such as the large plant-eater **Stegosaurus** [STEG-oh-SORE-us].

Allosauruses sometimes ate each other!

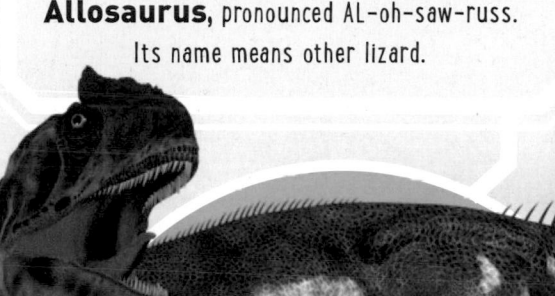

CRETACEOUS KINGS

By the end of the Cretaceous period, dinosaurs could be found on all seven continents. Dinosaurs had quickly adapted to their different habitats and their numbers had grown significantly. Dinosaurs were ruling the Earth!

Flowering plants began to grow during this time. The Earth came alive with colour! Dinosaurs started to share their world with **flying reptiles** - the pterosaurs.

This gigantic beast is **Argentinosaurus**, pronounced AR-gent-eeno-sore-us. Its name means Argentina lizard.

Two big Cretaceous beasts lived side by side. Argentinosaurus was a plant-eater, **43 m in length**. The meat-eating Giganotosaurus was **13 m long**, more than **3 times smaller!**

The **temperature** on Earth at the beginning of the Cretaceous period was much like the Jurassic period. Over the next few million years the temperature **cooled**.

Velociraptor [vel-OSS-ee-rap-tor] **was a vicious Cretaceous hunter.** Its name means speedy thief. Small, light and agile, Velociraptor was **built for speed,** which it needed to catch its prey. It's **bite was as powerful as a lion's!**

This hadrosaur is **Parasaurolophus,** pronounced pa-ra-saw-ROL-off-us. Its name means crested lizard.

This ankylosaur is **Euoplocephalus,** pronounced you-OH-plo-kef-ah-luss. Its name means well-armoured head.

Ankylosaurs were Cretaceous dinosaurs that were **built for defence.** They were covered in **spikes** and **horns.** Euoplocephalus even had special neck armour: several bony plates fused together in an arch-shaped block.

Hadrosaurs were the most common Cretaceous dinosaurs. They often had **strange head shapes** and odd-looking crests, possibly to **identify** members of their own species.

Large herds of dinosaurs like **Parasaurolophus** thrived during the Cretaceous period.

BIG AND SMALL

Plant-eaters, meat-eaters, big and small — there was a huge **variety of dinosaurs**. Some dinosaurs, like Diplodocus, could reach up to eat the leaves at the top of very tall trees. Others, like Microraptor, were as small as a bird!

This gigantic beast is **Diplodocus**, pronounced DIP-low DOCK-us. Its name means double beam.

Diplodocus had the **longest tail** of all the dinosaurs, up to **13 m in length**. That's longer than a bus!

Diplodocus weighed **20,000 kg** and was **26 m long** - that's the length of a **tennis court**!

The **biggest fossilised dinosaur bone** discovered is a thigh bone from a sauropod. It was found in Argentina and was **2.4 m long**! This one bone is taller than the tallest basketball player!

Mamenchisaurus [mah-men-chi-sore-us] was a **sauropod** with a **very long neck**. It was **9 m long**. A **giraffe**'s neck is just **under 2 m**.

This little feathered dinosaur is **Microraptor**, pronounced MIKE-row-rap-tor. Its name means tiny plunderer.

Another sauropod, **Sauroposeidon** [Sore-o-ps-sy-don] had the **longest neck** at **12 m long**. That's about the same length as **10 cars**!

Theropods were meat-eaters that walked on two legs. The most famous of all, **Tyrannosaurus rex**, had short arms for its body size. It measured **12 m long** but its **arms** were only **a metre in length**. That's about the size of a five-year-old!

Microraptor was a small feathered, winged dinosaur. It was only the size of a **pigeon**! It lived on a diet of **insects** and may have glided between trees hunting for them.

Giganotosaurus [gig-an-OH-toe-SORE-us] was the one of the **biggest meat-eaters**. It was a terrifying **12.5 m long**. That's as long as **one-and-a-half buses**!

Stegosaurus was the **size of a van** but it had the **smallest brain** of all the dinosaurs - about the size of a **walnut**.

Pentaceratops [pent-ah-ker-ah-tops] had one of the **biggest dinosaur heads** - about **3 m long**. That's as long as an **African elephant** is tall!

HOW DID THE DINOSAURS LIVE?

We will never really know everything about dinosaur life but their **fossilised remains** can give us some clues. Scientists have to carefully chip away at the rock surrounding the fossil before they can investigate what dinosaur it came from, what it looked like, what it ate and how it lived.

A large number of fossilised dinosaur eggs and nests have been found. Dinosaurs, like reptiles today, laid eggs, which came in all shapes and sizes. Some dinosaurs probably laid their eggs and left them to **hatch**. Other dinosaurs may have **looked after** their eggs and babies once they were born.

Bone beds that reveal huge numbers of fossilised dinosaur bones can shed some light, and certainly get scientists asking questions about the **lives of dinosaurs**. How did so many dinosaurs end up in one place? Was it a herd of dinosaurs that became trapped and died? Was there a drought in the area?

Fossilised poo can offer a big **insight** into the diet of a dinosaur. Triceratops bones have been found in the remains of **T. rex dung**!

This dinosaur is **Maiasaura**, pronounced my-ah-SORE-ah. Its name means good mother reptile.

Maiasaura is often seen as one of the most **nurturing** dinosaurs as it is thought that it **stayed with its young** when they hatched.

Maiasaura lived during the Late Cretaceous period in **enormous herds** - adults, juveniles and hatchlings all together. This offered **protection** from meat-eater's like **Troodon** [TROH-oh-don].

Fossil finds show Maiasaura laid between **30 and 40 eggs** at a time. Each one was about the same size as an **ostrich egg**.

It's possible the **eggs** were kept **warm** by using old **plant material** in the **nest**.

A female **Orodromeus** [or-oh-DROM-ee-us] laid about **12 eggs in a spiral**. When they hatched, the hatchlings were almost as fully developed as adults and could leave the nest and feed themselves.

A fossil of a nesting **Oviraptor** [OH-vee-RAP-tor] was discovered with two Velociraptor skulls nearby. Was this Oviraptor protecting its eggs?

19

BETTER TOGETHER

Some dinosaurs lived in **herds** or **groups**. This would have helped plant-eaters keep an eye out for predators. Meat-eaters could work together to take down larger prey, too.

This long-necked beast is **Puertasaurus**, pronounced PWER-tah-sore-us. Its name means Puerta's lizard

Many animals today, such as zebra, live together in groups for **protection**. Scientists think some plant-eating **sauropods** lived in **herds**, too. **There was safety in numbers!**

Some herds of sauropods may have **migrated long distances** in search of **food**. This is because they were **so big** they needed to **eat** the weight of a **small car in plants** every day!

Puertasaurus was about **38 m long**. That's the same as **three-and-a-half buses**!

Fossil finds tell us that **Corythosaurus** [koh-rith-OH-sore-us] had a **hollow crest** on its head. It may have used it to make a **noise**, like a trumpet, to **warn the herd of danger**.

Plant-eating **Tenontosaurus** [ten-ON-toe-sore-us] was one of the most common dinosaurs of the Cretaceous period. A **herd** was probably made up of many dinosaurs living together for **protection**. They could swing their very long tail at predators during an attack. Their tail was half their total 7-m body length!

While many **meat-eaters** hunted or scavenged alone, some, such as Deinonychus [die-NON-i-kuss], might have **hunted in packs**, like **lions**. This would have made it easier to take down large prey, such as Tenontosaurus.

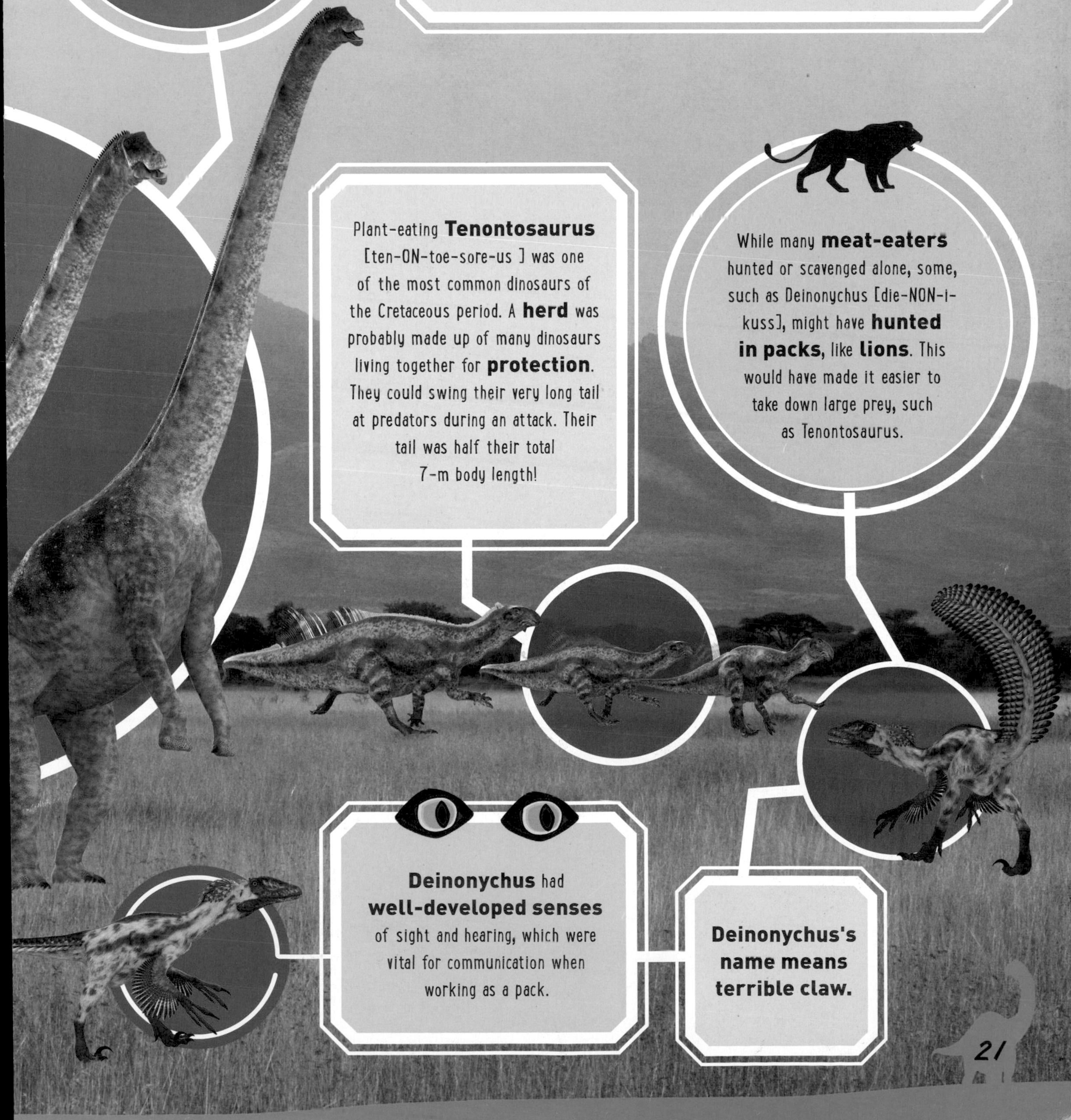

Deinonychus had **well-developed senses** of sight and hearing, which were vital for communication when working as a pack.

Deinonychus's name means terrible claw.

ATTACK

Meat-eating dinosaurs needed to **hunt** or **scavenge** food to survive. These **predators** had characteristics that made them excellent hunters.

Super senses such as excellent eyesight and a keen sense of smell helped meat-eaters **track down** their prey.

Meat-eaters had the **biggest brains** of the dinosaurs. They used their intelligence to process information and plan attacks.

Meat-eaters' **skin** probably mimicked the colour of their surroundings to allow them to **hide unseen** by their prey and strike when ready.

This scary dinosaur is **Allosaurus**.

Hunters needed **sharp teeth** and **claws** to catch their prey. **Allosaurus** teeth were up to **10 cm** long. This is quite small compared to **T. rex** teeth, which were **23 cm long** – about as long as a banana!

DEFENCE

Most dinosaurs were **plant-eaters**. Many were also a meat-eater's **prey**. They had all sorts of special features that protected them during an attack.

A sauropod's size was its best defence. Plant-eating **Barosaurus** [BAR-oh-sore-us] would have reached the top of a five-storey building when on its back legs.

Many plant-eating dinosaurs had **whip-like tails** to strike their attackers. Some even had extra spikes or clubs, such as **Ankylosaurus** [an-KIE-loh-sore-us]. One blow from its tail could disable even the biggest of meat-eaters.

Their **skin colour** might have helped them **blend into the background**.

Tough skin protected prey from a predator's sharp teeth.

This spiky dinosaur is **Stegosaurus**, pronounced STEG-oh-SORE-us, its name means roof lizard.

Spines, **scutes** and **bony plates** all over their body protected many dinosaurs from a meat-eater's sharp teeth and strong jaws. **Scelidosaurus** [skel-EYE-doh-sore-us] was covered in bony plates, called scutes. The scutes were strong enough to snap a predator's teeth!

Stegosaurus had **spikes** at the end of its tail. Fossil finds of these tail spikes are often damaged, suggesting they may have been harmed during an **attack**.

23

THE END OF THE DINOSAURS

Sixty-five million years ago, dinosaurs **disappeared** from the face of the Earth. What happened to them? There are a number of theories but no one is really sure.

Towards the end of the Cretaceous periods, volcanoes were erupting more and more frequently. It's possible a series of **volcanic eruptions** sent so much dust and ash into the air it **blocked out sunlight** on Earth. All animals need sunlight. Without sunlight, there wouldn't have been any plants, so no food for the plant-eaters and once they died out, no food for the carnivores.

Or could **climate change** be to blame? Did too much carbon dioxide build up and prevent the Sun's heat from escaping? This might have made Earth **too hot** to sustain life.

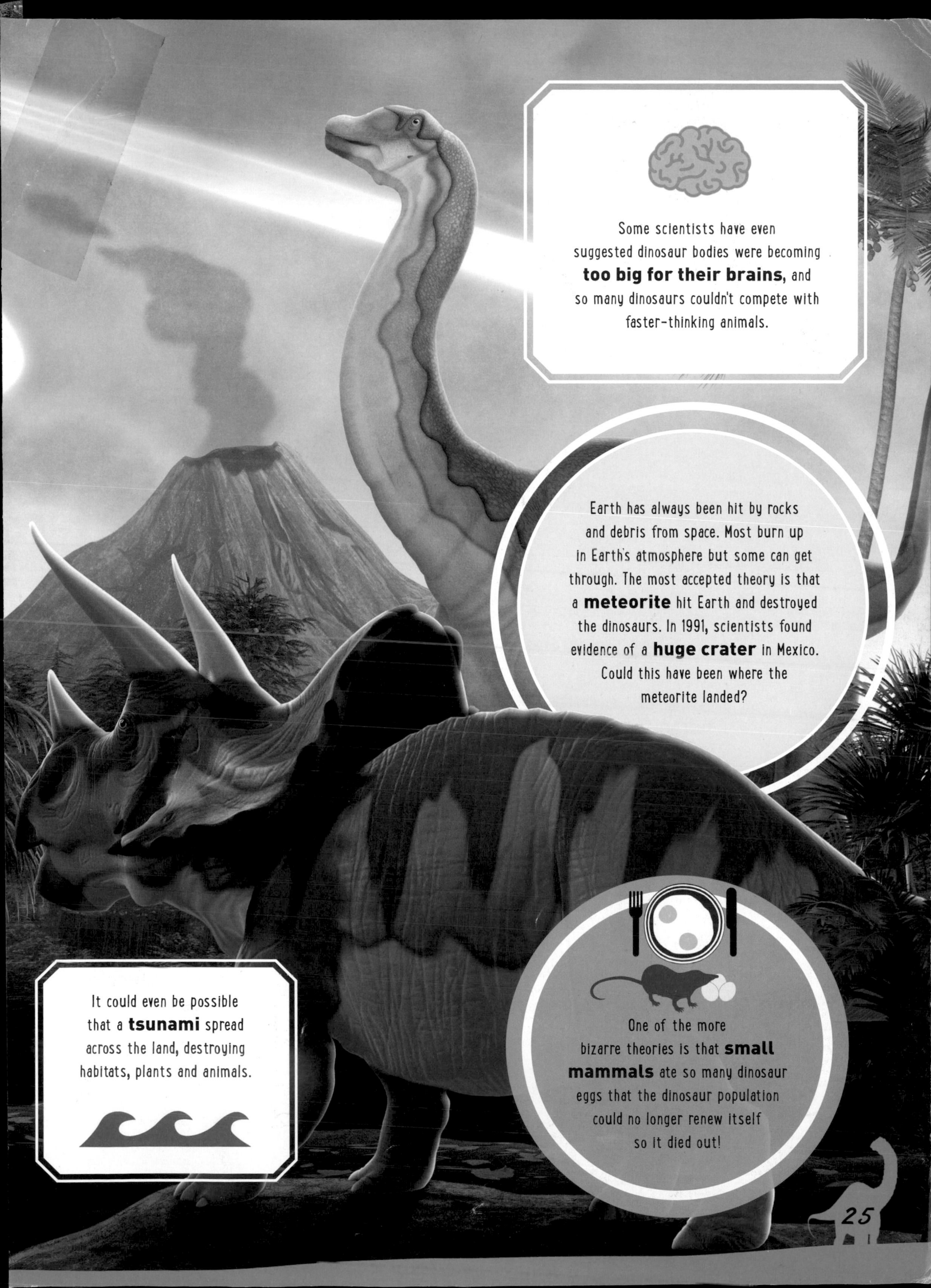

Some scientists have even suggested dinosaur bodies were becoming **too big for their brains,** and so many dinosaurs couldn't compete with faster-thinking animals.

Earth has always been hit by rocks and debris from space. Most burn up in Earth's atmosphere but some can get through. The most accepted theory is that a **meteorite** hit Earth and destroyed the dinosaurs. In 1991, scientists found evidence of a **huge crater** in Mexico. Could this have been where the meteorite landed?

It could even be possible that a **tsunami** spread across the land, destroying habitats, plants and animals.

One of the more bizarre theories is that **small mammals** ate so many dinosaur eggs that the dinosaur population could no longer renew itself so it died out!

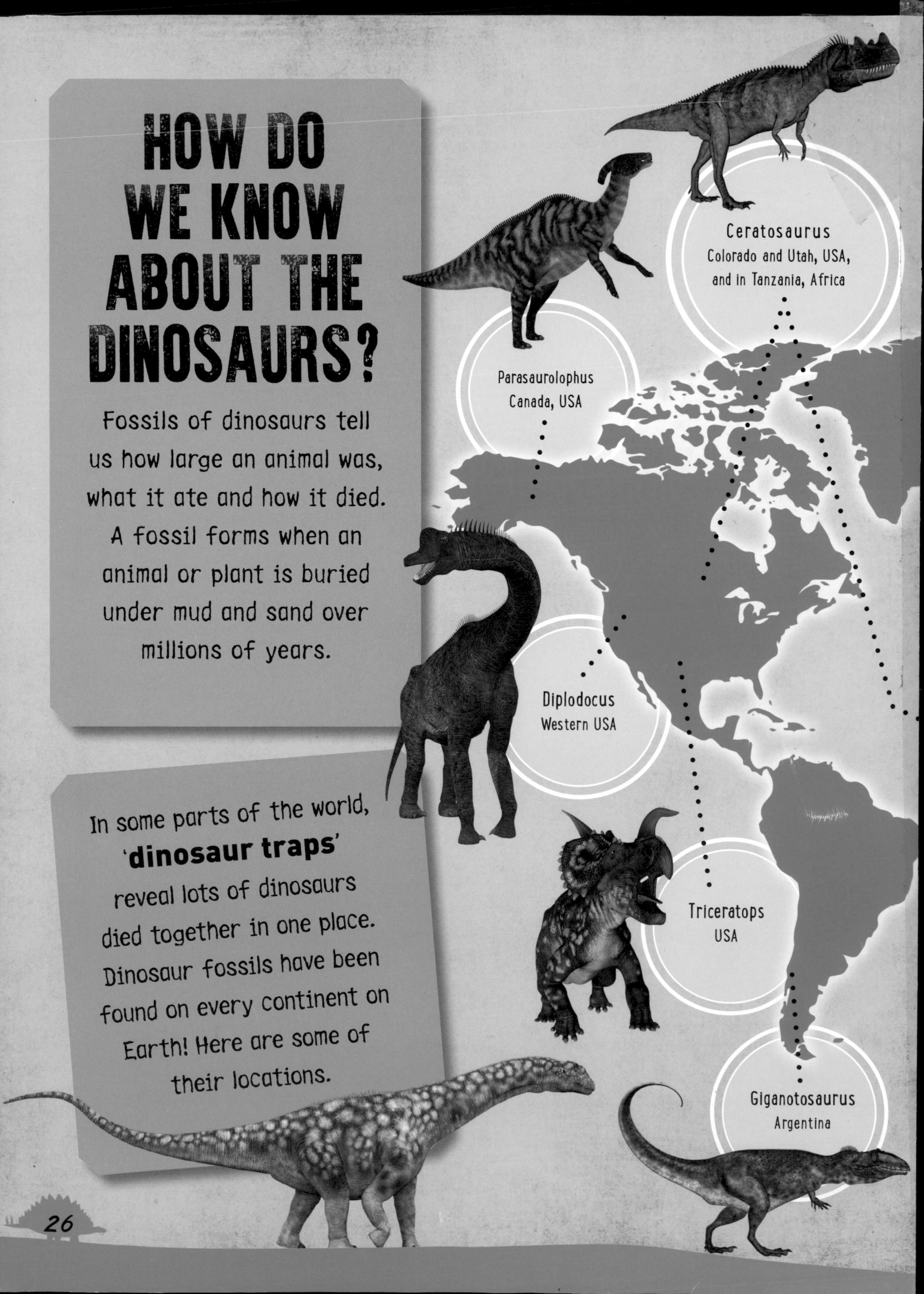

HOW DO WE KNOW ABOUT THE DINOSAURS?

Fossils of dinosaurs tell us how large an animal was, what it ate and how it died. A fossil forms when an animal or plant is buried under mud and sand over millions of years.

In some parts of the world, **'dinosaur traps'** reveal lots of dinosaurs died together in one place. Dinosaur fossils have been found on every continent on Earth! Here are some of their locations.

Ceratosaurus
Colorado and Utah, USA, and in Tanzania, Africa

Parasaurolophus
Canada, USA

Diplodocus
Western USA

Triceratops
USA

Giganotosaurus
Argentina

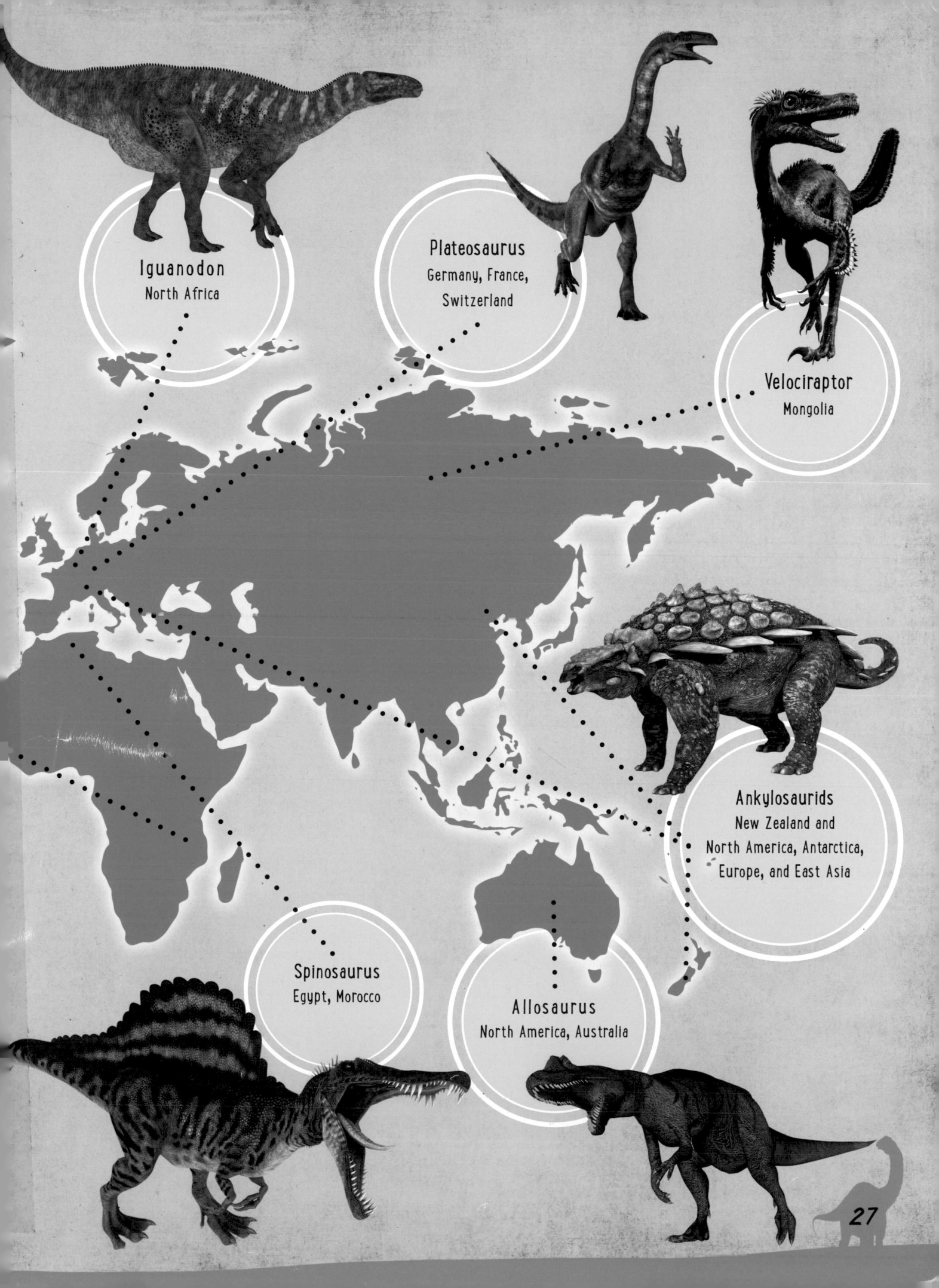

Iguanodon
North Africa

Plateosaurus
Germany, France,
Switzerland

Velociraptor
Mongolia

Ankylosaurids
New Zealand and
North America, Antarctica,
Europe, and East Asia

Spinosaurus
Egypt, Morocco

Allosaurus
North America, Australia

DINOSAURS TODAY

The best place to find out about dinosaurs is at your nearest **natural history museum**. You can also look up in the sky ... Did you know that modern birds are the descendants of dinosaurs?

Not all creatures died out with the dinosaurs. It's possible to find examples of prehistoric life all around us today. Modern-day **crocodiles, sharks** and **jellyfish** have barely changed from the time of the dinosaurs.

The discovery of **'dino-birds'**, such as **Sinosauropteryx** [sine-oh-sore-op-ter-iks] and **Archaeopteryx** [ark-ee-OPT-er-ix], has led scientists to think that **dinosaurs are related to birds**.

Some **modern birds** still have **clawed wings** like some dinosaurs. **Hoatzin chicks** have two tiny claws on each wing tip.

MORE DINO FACTS

TROODON

LENGTH: 2 m

WEIGHT: 40 kg

DIET: Small mammals and reptiles

LIVED: Late Cretaceous period

FIRST FOSSIL DISCOVERY Montana, USA in 1855

FACT: Troodon had the largest brain of any dinosaur, relative to its body size.

STEGOSAURUS

LENGTH: 9 m

WEIGHT: 2,400 kg

DIET: Plants

LIVED: Late Jurassic period

FIRST FOSSIL DISCOVERY: Colorado, USA in 1903

FACT: Stegosaurus' bony plates may have blushed red when blood rushed to them!

COMPSOGNATHUS

LENGTH: 65 cm

WEIGHT: 3.6 kg

DIET: Lizards

LIVED: Jurassic period

FIRST FOSSIL DISCOVERY: Bavaria, Germany 1859

FACT: Compsognathus was only the size of a chicken, but it was still a fierce predator.

SAUROPOSEIDON

LENGTH: 30 m

WEIGHT: 60,000 kg

DIET: Plants

LIVED: Cretaceous period

FIRST FOSSIL DISCOVERY: Oklahoma, USA in 1999

FACT: Reached 18 m high. It could easily peer into a six-storey window!

GLOSSARY

adapt to adjust to a new environment

bone bed an area of rock that contains bones of fossilised animals

carbon dioxide a gas without colour or odour that is made up of carbon and oxygen. It is in the air.

carnivore an animal that eats meat

climate change the average climate of the Earth. This includes temperature, winds and other factors. Scientists are concerned that the Earth is warming up very fast.

conifer a kind of tree

continent one of the seven major areas of land on Earth

crater a hole on the surface (of Earth or the Moon, for example) made by something enormous hitting it, such as a meteorite

crest a growth of feathers, flesh or bone on the head of an animal

Cretaceous period a period in Earth's history, between 144 and 65 million years ago

descendant someone or something that is descended from an ancestor

dinosaur trap an area with lots of dinosaur fossils

dominate to be more powerful than others

drought a long period without water. Animals, plants and people need water to survive.

evolve to develop, change or improve by steps

food chain a group of animals and plants that rely on one another as a source of food

fossil the remains of an animal or plant, preserved for millions of years

habitat the place where an animal or a plant lives

hadrosaurs a group of plant-eating dinosaurs that lived during the Late Cretaceous period. They walked on two legs, had a beak-like snout and often had a bony crest on their heads.

hatchling a young animal that has recently come out from its egg

herbivore an animal that eats plants

Jurassic period a period of Earth's history, between 206 and 144 million years ago

juvenile a young or baby animal

Mesozoic Era a period of time in Earth's history from 251 to 65 million years ago.

meteorite a piece of rock that falls from space

migrate to travel from one area to another in the search of food or due to the seasons

Pangaea one big continent on the Earth. Pangaea included all the present seven continents joined together, before they broke up and drifted apart.

predator an animal that eats other animals

prey an animal that is eaten by another animal

quarry a hole in the ground from which something can be removed

reptile a cold-blooded animal that breathes air and is usually covered in scales

sauropods a group of dinosaurs that walked on four legs, had long tails and necks, small heads and thick, column-shaped limbs

scute a thick bony plate on the back of an animal

theropods a group of meat-eating dinosaurs

tsunami a large ocean wave caused by an underwater volcanic eruption or earthquake

volcanic eruption the sudden expulsion of steam and volcanic material

Triassic period a period in Earth's history, between 248 and 206 million years ago.

FURTHER INFORMATION

Further Reading

Dinosaurs A Children's Encyclopaedia by DK (DK Children, 2011)

Children's Dinosaur Atlas by John Malam (QED Publishing, 2017)

Planet Earth: Birth of the Dinosaurs by Michael Bright (Wayland, 2016)

Websites

www.nhm.ac.uk/discover/dino-directory/timeline/late-triassic/gallery.html

www.bbc.co.uk/sn/prehistoric_life/dinosaurs/

www.theguardian.com/science/dinosaurs

INDEX